Vivekananda

Padmavathi Vajjulu

Vivekananda

© *New Horizon Media*

First Edition: March 2009
64 Pages
Printed in India.

ISBN 978–81–8493–092–4
Pro–ya–en–34

Prodigy Books
177/103, First Floor, Ambal's Building
Lloyds Road, Royapettah, Chennai 600 014.
Ph: +91-44-4200-9603
Email: support@nhm.in
Website: www.nhm.in

Prodigy Books is an imprint of New Horizon Media Pvt. Ltd.

Contents

Incredible India

INDIA—say this magical word and a feeling of intense pride fills one's mind, heart and soul. Every individual who is an Indian by birth, by heart and by choice says it's a beautiful feeling to be a part of such a vast country which represents unity in diversity.

'Unity in diversity', is not just another phrase or quotation for a country like India. It is a true reflection of India that is incredibly rich in culture and heritage. The culture of India happens to be one of the oldest. Yet one can see an amazing cultural diversity through out the country which makes it different from the rest of the world. India is home to some of the most ancient civilizations, including four major world religions – Hinduism, Buddhism, Jainism and Sikhism. Apart from

the traditions, religions and castes, a combination of various factors like humanity, tolerance, unity, secularism and a closely knit social system has resulted in an exclusive culture – Indian culture.

India is the home of Philosophy, Religion and Spirituality. Every age, she provides the world with spiritual masters to enlighten the world about life. The major religion in India, *Hinduism*, is ancient and is considered to be the mother of all religions. Though the most ancient of all religions, it is quite modern in its thinking. This adaptive nature of the religion, based on a firm foundation, makes it vibrant.

There was, however, a time when India fell deep into a chasm of ignorance, grief, confusion and restlessness. Before people could notice, they sank deeper and deeper into a state of misery. It is often said that God has ways of leading his dearest ones to the light. He has His own plans of destruction, revival and destiny. He sends His men to bring the world out of its hardships.

One such great soul and a teacher came to the rescue when India was rapidly falling into traps of ignorance. He traveled all over India, studied the worst conditions prevailing then, took the trouble to think, re-think and to act relentlessly in order to regain the lost glory of India.

He believed that when a nation goes down and shatters into pieces, God would send His messenger to raise the nation up again. The messenger of God would use all his power to revive the nation and virtues bring back into the society.

He might not have known then, that for Indians and in fact for the whole world, 'the messenger of God' he spoke about was none other than himself. He presented the world with a positive view of the human individual. He always raised the spirits of those around him by saying 'Ignorance is less knowledge' and 'We do not move from falsehood to truth – we move from lesser truth to higher truth.'

He was a majestic figure with a commanding presence, vast learning, deep insight and above all, a great teacher. He believed in education and pronounced it to be the best way to achieve perfection and knowledge of your true self. He believed in the Socratic teaching 'Knowledge is virtue.' He, who was a driving force to evolve a new India and bring back to Mother India her lost glory, was none other than **SWAMI VIVEKANANDA** – a great thinker, spiritual teacher and a saint.

Birth and Early Life

Born on 12 January 1863, in ShimlaPally, Kolkata, Vivekananda belonged to an orthodox, affluent Hindu family. His parents, Viswanath Datta and Bhuvaneswari Devi originally named him Narendranath Dutta and called him Naren affectionately.

His father, Viswanath Datta was a brilliant lawyer who was a modern liberal thinker and had a scientific outlook to life. He was highly respected for his intelligence and culture. Viswanath Datta had scholarly discussions with his clients and friends on various topics like religion, science and politics. From when he was very young, Naren showed interest in the debates held at his house. He also showed he was capable of independent thinking. Viswanath Datta encouraged Naren to participate in

Bhuvaneshwari Devi

the discussions held in his house. Equally enthusiastic, Naren never showed any hesitation to join his father and friends in such discussions and debates. He was never embarrassed to voice out his opinions about whatever he thought was right. He also used to advance suitable arguments to support his stand on every matter of discussion held.

A few of Viswanath Datta's friends disliked Naren's presence amongst them and they openly resented his guts and audacity to debate and discuss matters concerning adults. To this, Naren would always say, 'Point out where I am wrong but why should you object to my independent thinking?' It was this fearless, straight-forward nature which made Naren special from other kids his age.

Viswanath Datta was liberal minded, but he was always skeptical about religious practices. He never displayed any interest towards worship and other rituals. On the other hand, Bhuvaneswari Devi was a pious lady, who followed all the Hindu traditions. She believed in worship and devotedly followed all religious practices. She inspired virtues of fearlessness, honesty, justice and devotion in Naren.

As a child, Naren was naughty, brave, fearless and self willed. He was generous, loving and devoted with a strange attraction to *sadhus*. He possessed fantastic sense of humour. From a very early age, he never approved of any kind of injustice. He was always ready to help people who were in need. Though he was a sweet boy, he was a bit unruly as well. He was so full of mischief that his parents had to employ two nurses to keep him constantly under check. At times, to quiet little Naren, his mother would put his head under the tap, turn on the cold water and make him repeat the name of Lord Shiva continuously. This treatment strangely calmed Naren down.

Naren bore a striking resemblance to his grandfather, DurgaCharan, who renounced the world in search of God and chose to lead a monastic life after the birth of his first child. Not only did he physically resemble DurgaCharan, Naren was also attracted to monks which made people think DurgaCharan was reborn as his grandson. In fact, his attraction to wandering monks was so great that the mere sight of a monk would excite him and he forgot everything around him immediately.

One day a monk came to Naren's house seeking alms. Naren was so excited on seeing him that he gave away a new cloth that was wrapped around his waist without any hesitation. Since then, whenever a monk was seen wandering around in the neighborhood, Naren would be locked up in a room till the monk went away. Even then, he used to sit by the window and throw anything at hand as an offering to the monk.

Naren was sent to school like all the other children for his primary education when he turned six. He happened to pick up a few vulgar words at school, and his parents decided not to send him to school anymore. They engaged a private tutor to educate him at home for some time.

Naren displayed two peculiar tendencies since a very tender age. The first was the ability to go into intense meditation with ease and the second was the capacity of intense mental concentration due to which he remembered subject matter of books just by reading them once. His tutor was very surprised to find him memorize Sanskrit grammar and long passages from Ramayana and Mahabharata easily by reading them once.

One day he was in meditation along with some of his friends in a room. Suddenly, a cobra appeared and slithered across the floor. All the children ran away. Naren who was engrossed in his meditation neither noticed the snake nor heard the hue and cry of his friends. Such was the remarkable power of concentration he possessed which detached him from everything else while he was concentrating.

Little Naren often wondered why one human being was considered superior to another. He noticed different tobacco pipes in his father's office for clients of different castes. As per the custom that prevailed then, the pipe that was meant for Muslim clients was kept apart from the rest. Intrigued by this difference in treatment, Naren smoked tobacco from all the pipes including from that which was marked for Muslims. Later when he was reprimanded by his parents for smoking, he answered.

that he smoked to find out why separate pipes were kept for clients of different castes and religions and also told them that he could not find any difference in the tobacco in all the pipes that were there. Though still a child, he always tried to find a logical reason for the way things were done and would accept them only if he was convinced thoroughly with the logic he found.

It was during these formative years that his future personality was greatly influenced by his parents. They always kept an eye on him, checked his actions and behaviour constantly. His father was not strict but he had his own way of instilling discipline in Naren. In one particular instance, Viswanath Datta overheard Naren passing rude remarks on his mother in the heat of an argument. He did not scold Naren directly. Instead, he wrote on the door of Naren's room with charcoal that he had abused his mother and also wrote all words he used. He wanted Naren's friends to know how rudely he had behaved with his mother.

At the age of seven, Naren entered high school. He was recognized as an academic genius and he also excelled at various games. He organized an amateur theatrical company, a gymnasium, took lessons in fencing, wrestling, rowing and other sports. He was much sought after by people due to his various accomplishments. He was everyone's favourite and people admired him for his straightforward nature and simplicity. He was also a bold and a fearless lad for his age and often used to tell his friends not to believe what others said until they had checked its authenticity themselves. He also has great presence of mind and courage that enabled him to handle difficult situations.

An incident where his courage can be highlighted happened when he was still in school. Naren and his friends decided to set up a heavy trapeze in the gymnasium one day and sought the help of people who were present there. An English sailor came forward to help them, and during the process of moving the trapeze, it crashed down on the sailor and made him unconscious. All those who were present there, ran away afraid that the man was dead. They did not want to be caught by police. Naren stayed there, administered first aid to the injured man and revived him. He also took him to the schoolhouse, nursed him for a week and sent him away with some money he had collected from his friends.

Apart from all the talents and virtues he had, Naren was also a master story teller. He narrated stories in such an interesting manner that people around him got engrossed in his stories. One day in school, Naren started talking to his friends during the interval. Being the orator he was, all the students were soon engrossed in what Naren was saying. Meanwhile, the teacher entered the classroom and resumed his lessons. The students were too absorbed in Naren's story to listen to the lessons. After a while, the teacher heard a few whispers and was annoyed that no one was paying attention to him. He asked each student to tell him what he had been lecturing on. All of them failed to answer, which only made him angrier. When the teacher asked Naren to repeat what he had been lecturing about, Naren promptly delivered every minute detail of the teacher's lecture. The teacher was amazed at the correctness of his reply and asked the students to tell him who had been talking continuously while he lectured. All the students pointed to Naren but the teacher refused to believe them.

As he was unable to get satisfactory answers from the students, the teacher asked all the students except Naren to stand up on the bench for the rest of the period. Naren also stood up on the bench. When the teacher asked him to sit down, he immediately replied, 'No Sir, I must also stand because it was I who was talking to them.' This incident shows us how truthful and sincere Naren was, and his fearlessness with regard to owning up to his mistakes at the cost of his own comfort. All the virtues he displayed from a very tender age stayed with him forever and made him a great man who showed the world a new and a better way of living.

In 1879, after his matriculation, Naren went to college. He joined the Presidency College, Calcutta. One year later, he joined the Scottish Church College, then known as General Assembly's Institution, to study philosophy. He passed his B.A from the Scottish Church College. He was rarely absent from social parties. He was the **'soul of social circles'** and no gathering was considered complete without his presence.

The versatile young Naren had a sharp intellect and read literature from both the East and the West. This included Western philosophy and the great English poets. He was well versed with both Indian and western philosophical thought, including the Vedanta of Upanishads and newer trends in the philosophy in European culture. He particularly liked the rational reasoning of the West and was upset to find many religious superstitions that prevailed in India brought about the cultural decline in the Indian society.

He was a rare combination of man who had equal quest for science and literature. He was hungry for knowledge in all the fields. He once even went to Calcutta Medical School to see for himself the arrangement of brain, spinal cord, and the nerves in the bodies in the anatomical museum to understand the flow of current in the body so that he could relate them to various *Kundalini Chakras* present in the body that are mentioned in *Vedas*.

He was equally talented in music and singing. His voice was clear, pure, and so full of emotion that was sure to bring tears to the eyes of the listeners. He was an expert in playing instruments like *tabla*, *mrudungam*, and especially the *pakhavaz*.

As a student of philosophy, doubts and questions regarding the presence of God were always there in his mind. He often questioned himself as to was there a God? If there was a God, what was he like? What were man's relations with him? and so on. He discussed these questions with many people, but no one could clarify his doubts satisfactorily. He constantly looked for people who could say they had seen God, but found none. It was then that he was drawn to join the Brahmo Samaj, an important religious movement at that time, led by Keshub Chander Sen. Keshub was a great orator and many young people were attracted to his oratory skills and enrolled themselves in Brahmo Samaj. Naren was one among them.

The Brahmo Samaj sought to revitalise Indian life and spirituality through a rationalistic approach and it focused mainly on abandoning image worship. Naren, and his friend Brajendra Nath Seal regularly attended the meetings of the Samaj. For a while, he was satisfied with what the Brahmo Samaj taught him, but he soon began to feel it did not provide him with answers where religion was concerned. The meetings, prayers and devotional songs could neither quench his thirst to realize God nor his quest for knowledge. It was during this period that Reverend William Hastie, the principal of Scottish Church College, told him about Sri Ramakrishna of Dakshineswar.

Association of a Great Guru

Naren met Ramakrishna for the first time in November 1881. One day, his neighbour received a surprise visit from the saint of Dakshineshwar, Sri Ramakrishna. Naren was invited to sing devotional songs. As he sang, Sri Ramakrishna fell into a state of ecstasy. When he became normal again, he made Naren sit beside him and enquired lovingly of the boy. Ramakrishna invited him to visit Dakshineswar at his earliest convenience.

Sri Ramakrishna had not particularly created any impression during their first meeting. Though he was invited to Dakshineswar, he hardly thought of visiting the place to meet Sri Ramakrishna. As the days passed, he began to grow restless regarding the various riddles that religion presented.

Naren then decided to visit Dakshineswar along with his friends to meet Sri Ramakrishna. On seeing Naren at the Kali temple, Sri Ramakrishna immediately got up and said 'O Narayana, why did you take such long to come here? I have been restlessly waiting for you for long.'

Saying this, he escorted him to an inner room and fed him sweets and other eatables with his own hands. He treated Naren with utmost love and affection. This puzzled Naren immensely and he did not wish to visit Sri Ramakrishna again.

He postponed his second visit to Dakshineswar for six months. He thought him to be a simple, insane Brahmin. In spite of all his reservations, logical reasoning and skepticism, Naren could not resist visiting Sri Ramakrishna for the second time.

Sri Ramakrishna was sitting all alone. He was very pleased to receive Naren and called him near his tiny bedstead. Sri Ramakrishna touched Naren's body with his right foot. Immediately Naren experienced something wonderful.

He saw that all the things in the room were together with the walls rapidly whirling and receding into an unknown region. He was overwhelmed by a terrible fear and thought that death was before him. Unable to

Ramakrishna Paramahamsa

control himself, he cried out loudly, 'Ah! What is it you have done to me? I have my parents, you know.'

Laughing at his words, Sri Ramakrishna touched Naren's chest with his hand and said, 'Let it cease then. It need not be done all at once. It will come to pass in course of time.' Naren was amazed to notice that he came to a state of normalcy and saw things as they were before. He then thought, 'How could I consider this person mad, when he can shatter the structure of a mind like mine to pieces.'

The third visit was much sooner than the second one. This time, Sri Ramakrishna asked Naren to accompany him to the nearby garden of Jadu Mallick. Naren and Sri Ramakrishna were left alone there. Sri Ramakrishna went into an ecstatic mood and elevated Naren to such a state of consciousness where although Naren forgot himself bodily, he could still answer the questions put forward by Sri Ramakrishna.

Sri Ramakrishna asked Naren the purpose of his descent on the earth, the nature of his work in the future, his plans and mission in life and so on. On the basis of these questions he came to know that Naren would lead a monk's life and would leave his body when he comes to know his true nature.

Though Naren could not accept Ramakrishna and his visions, he could not neglect him either. He started to visit Ramakrishna frequently, as it had always been in Naren's nature to test something thoroughly before he would accept it. He tested Ramakrishna to the maximum with silly and illogical doubts and questions that arose in his mind, but the master was patient, forgiving, humorous, and full of love. He never asked Naren to abandon reason, and he faced Naren's arguments and examinations with patience.

Naren loved and admired Sri Ramakrishna, but he never surrendered his independence of judgement. Neither did Sri Ramakrishna nor any of his other disciples demanded it from him. As his intimacy with Sri Ramakrishna grew, Naren was forced to change many of his preconceived notions about God, divinity, and perfected souls. He started to build faith in Ramakrishna and accepted him. When he accepted, his acceptance was whole-hearted.

Naren was about twenty one years of age and everything was going on smoothly for him at home and at Dakshineswar, when his father suddenly died due to a massive heart attack. Vishwanath Dutta, although outwardly appeared well off, was in severe debt. His unusual generosity and carelessness in handling money-matters had put him in a situation where there were no savings left. Hearing the news of his death, the debtors took away their share leaving the bereaved family in utter poverty. Naren's uncles also shied away in this hour of crisis, and instead of helping him they took away their share of the property and avoided Naren's family. His father's death came as a rude shock to Naren. It was a life shattering incident for him. He had to take the responsibility of the family after his father, and it was difficult for him to make two ends meet.

Even after many trials, Naren could not get a job. One day, he decided to leave home and walk in the unknown world as a *Sannyasin*. At Dakshineswar, Sri Ramakrishna, in one of his spiritual moods, came to know of his beloved disciple's secret resolve to leave the world, and was anguished and concerned about Naren's decision.

Sri Ramakrishna met Naren in one of his devotee's house. In his deep emotional voice, the Master sang a song:

'I am afraid to speak, and equally afraid not to speak,
The doubt rises in my mind,
Lest I should lose you, ah my Rai,
Lest I should lose you'

Immediately after Sri Ramakrishna had finished singing, Naren understood the meaning of the song. He at once knew that Sri Ramakrishna had come to know of his secret resolve to become *Sannyasin*, and that the song was meant for him to reconsider his decision. Tears flowed down the cheeks of both the Guru and the disciple. When their emotions calmed down, Sri Ramakrishna forced Naren to accompany him to Dakshineswar. There, Sri Ramakrishna inquired about the problem and requested Naren not to desert him till his death. Narendra had to promise, for he could not disobey his Master.

Naren who was still worried about the well being of his family, asked Sri Ramakrishna to pray to Goddess Kali and ask her to supply his family with grain and clothes. *'I know the Mother listens to you and definitely grants your prayers'*, he told Sri Ramakrishna.

'Look my boy,' the Master replied. 'I have given everything to the Mother. How can I ask for anything back from her now? There is, however, one thing I can tell you. Why don't you go and pray to the Mother to fulfill your wish? My Mother is very kind and gracious and I am sure she will not disappoint you.'

Naren thus decided to pray to the Mother to fulfill his wants and he went to the Mother's shrine to pray and ask for material things of urgent necessity. However, as he entered the shrine, all that he could say was, 'O Mother, please give me *Jnana* and *Bhakti*.'

After the prayer, he came back to Sri Ramakrishna, who inquired, 'Naren, have you asked for food and money required for your family?'

Naren replied, 'Why, no sir! I asked for Jnana and Bhakti.'

'You fool,' said the Master, 'Go and ask for wealth and the things you actually need now.'

Thrice Naren went to Ma Kali, but could not utter a word about money, clothes, food, and grains, but instead all the three times he prayed to the Mother for Jnana and Bhakti!.

By now, Naren who was against idol worship understood the deeper meaning of his Master's word   that formless God and God with form as the Mother were but one. It was on that very day, he accepted Maa Kali as the highest embodiment of spiritual virtues, power, and knowledge. He bowed down at the holy feet of the Master and prayed, 'O Lord, today I came to know who you are. You are all, everything in this universe. I do not want anything anymore from the Mother. It is all your wish.'

Embracing Naren, he assured, 'Go my son, be at peace. From today onwards you and your family will be provided with simple clothes and food, and shelter. This much I guarantee you and your family.'

Sri Ramakrishna was Naren's anchor during his most difficult phase of life and taught him the most significant truths from the incidents that occurred in his own life. Not only was Sri Ramakrishna a Guru to Naren, he was also the embodiement of a divine soul who's descent to earth was with the specific purpose of spreading the message of harmony on earth.

During the five years of his training under Ramakrishna, Naren came to know the essence of religion as 'Realization of Highest Truth' in our lives.

In August 1886, Sri Ramakrishna was diagnosed with throat cancer. He was terminally ill. Naren organized a team of his fellow brothers and devotees to take care of the Master. Timetables were set up so that someone would always be available to provide Sri Ramakrishna and Ma Saradadevi any help. The household devotees offered monetary and material help for his nursing care, medicines, and food.

Naren had few doubts left in the heart of his hearts. One day, as he was sitting at the holy feet of his ailing Master, a thought arose in his mind, 'If now in this condition of distress the Master tells me he is Avatar Purusha, then I will accept him as the greatest of God Man.' As soon as the thought arose in his mind, Sri Ramakrishna, though weak and unable to get up, said,

'Even now you have doubts! O Naren, He who was Rama and He who was Krishna is now RamaKrishna in this body.' That message had completed the training, revelations, and transfer of all the spiritual powers from the master to his most able disciple for the welfare and benefit of future mankind. All doubts vanished from Naren's heart and mind. He had become one with the master.

Sri Ramakrishna left the worldly abode on 16 August 1886. He wanted Naren and a few other disciples to lead a monastic life and symbolically gave a gerua cloth (light orange robe). After the Master's death, Naren and a group of Ramakrishna's disciples took vows to become monks and renounce material life. As per his master's desire, Naren rented a supposedly haunted house in Baranagore and converted it into a monastery. The disciples took alms to satisfy their hunger and their other needs were taken care of by Ramakrishna's richer household disciples. They worshiped Sri Ramakrishna's photograph, read his teachings and his messages, and also read from the ancient Indian scriptures, the Gita and Upanishads everyday. The Ramakrishna Mission had come to life.

The Wandering Monk

Naren's knowledge remained confined in his heart, making him glow with divinity, but the condition of his mind was like a bird trapped in a golden cage. It wanted to spread its mighty wings, strengthened with the power of teachings of the Master, and fly far away. He heard an inner call to a greater mission. He desired to go into open world to learn more about the practicality of Vedanta. Many questions about how Vedanta could be applied in day-to-day life to alleviate the sufferings of the masses crowded his mind all day and night.

Finally one day, sometime in July 1888, Naren left Calcutta alone, telling his brother disciples not to follow him. Thus started the second important phase in the

Naren's life, that of the *Parivrajaka* Monk (the wandering monk). He went to all places of socio-religious importance like Varanasi, Ayodhya, Vrindavan, Lucknow, Agra, and the Himalayas, thus covering the entire north of India.

One day, when he was in the Himalayas, he saw an old man exhausted and standing hopelessly at the foot of an upward slope. When the man saw Naren, he said to him in frustration, 'Oh, Sir, how do I cross the Himalayas? If I walk any more, my chest will break.'

Naren listened to the old man patiently and then said, 'Look down at your feet. The road that is under your feet is the road that you have passed over and is the same road that you see before you; it will soon be under your feet.' These simple yet powerful words gave the old man reassurance and the power to resume his journey.

His trip to North India was short and he returned to Calcutta in a few months' time. For sometime he remained in the company of his brother disciples. It was during this time, he tried to devise the means and the ways to propagate Sri Ramakrishna's message to every nook and corner of the world. He had this intense desire to spread the wonderful message 'Divine Unity of Existence and Unity in Diversity.'

For the second time in around July 1890, he left his brothers to wander all over the country, after seeking blessings from Ma Saradadevi, Sri Ramakrishna's widow. For more than two years, he wandered all over India from North to West, West to South and during his wanderings, he assimilated and understood the socio-religious and economic conditions prevalent in India. During his wandering days, he stayed in kings' palaces, as well as the huts of the poor.

When he was young, Naren once asked his father 'How shall I conduct myself in the world?' Though it was a question which was vast in itself, his father without any hesitation advised him to 'Never show surprise at anything'. This advice given by Viswanath Datta immensely helped him to treat the luxurious king's palaces and the straw huts of the beggars alike. It helped him preserve his peace of mind irrespective of the place in which he stayed.

It saddened him to see India, the land of charity and prayers, drowning in ignorance and poverty. He swore to himself that he would restore the lost glory of the nation. As a first step towards his vow, he set out to visit holy places. He visited Gaya and went to Benares.

In Benares he had a revelation. He was coming out of a Durga temple after worship and suddenly he was surrounded by a large number of chattering monkeys. He was quite scared and began to runaway from them. The monkeys chased him. An old man who was there watching it all, called out to him and said 'Stop! Face the brutes!' Naren stopped, turned around and faced the monkeys. At once, they ran away. This incident gave him the strength to face the troubles in his incessant attempts to regain India's glory. Many years later, during one of his lectures, he quoted this incident and said, 'Do not run away from troubles, fools or death; face them, instead; only then will they vanish.'

He could understand and openly declare that the real cause of India's downfall was the neglect of the masses. The immediate need was to provide food and other bare necessities of life to the hungry millions. 'To the hungry religion comes in the form of bread.' he declared.

He understood that the downtrodden people of India needed secular knowledge to improve their economic condition and also spiritual knowledge to build faith in their abilities and to strengthen their moral senses. Soon, he wondered how to spread this knowledge among the masses? He was convinced that educating the masses was the only option to reform the society. He urged that science and religion should join hands so that a new chapter could be written in the human history. Material progress, secular education, and service to sick must be added to meditation and spiritual practices for fulfillment of final spiritual aim. He believed that one had to direct all his efforts to bridge the wide gap between material progress and spiritual uplift. It was clear to him that to carry out his plans for the spread of education and to uplift the poor and the women, an efficient organization of dedicated people was needed.

He met many eminent and noble persons, princes and intellectuals by traveling all over India. All those whom he met were highly impressed by the sincerity, knowledge, spirituality and the new Vedantic approach to life of this English speaking Monk, but they were too engrossed in their own affairs to take the swami's words seriously. They ignored his constant appeals to uplift the downtrodden masses.

Initially, he was shocked to see the indifference of the educated men towards the poor. He gradually began to know that all of them ignored him because he was only a 'wandering monk' and that the educated men in India were totally under the influence of thinkers from the West. They ceased to think on their own. This slave mentality of fellow Indians pained him immensely. He understood that they were too selfish to bother about the suffering in the society. Even then, he did not stop his trials to meet and ask help from eminent and famous people.With every trip, consciousness spread amongst the leaders and a slow change began to take place.

The Maharaja of Khetri, The Maharaja of Mysore, Dewan of Porbandar and Junagadh and the Raja of Ramnad were among the first few who promised to help him bring change in the existing conditions of the society. In fact, the ruler of Mysore was among the first to make primary education free within his State. This, however, was not enough for Naren. He wanted education taken to the peasant's door-step, so that the peasant's children could work and learn at the same time. He wanted 'to set in motion the machinery which will bring noblest ideas to the doorstep of even the poorest and the meanest.'

It was during these days, he assumed various names like Swami Satchidananda and Vividishananda. It is a wide belief that he was given the name Vivekananda by the Maharaja of Khetri for his discrimination of things, good and bad. Thus, Narendranath Datta became Swami Vivekananda.

Vivekananda reached Kanyakumari, the southernmost tip of the Indian subcontinent on 24 December 1892. He swam across the sea and meditated on a lone rock for three days on the past, present and future of India.

Vivekananda

The rock is today a primary tourist destination and is called the Vivekananda memorial.

Vivekananda went to Madras and spoke about his plans for India and Hinduism to the young men of Madras. They were impressed by him and felt that he was the right person to represent and elaborate the true Hinduism in the World Parliament of Religions that was to take place in Chicago. The Dewan of Porbandar too told Swami Vivekananda that he ought to go to the West where people will understand him and his worth. He expressed a hope that Swami Vivekananda could throw a great light on Western culture by preaching the Sanatana Dharma. They all urged him to go to the United States and represent Hinduism in the World Parliament of Religions. Though Swami Vivekananda was initially reluctant to go, he later agreed as he thought his visit to the West might be of some use to India, which proved to be right.

The Raja of Ramnad, who was originally invited for the conference, immediately agreed that Swami Vivekananda was the right person to represent Hinduism in the Parliament. The Maharaja of Khetri provided necessary funds for Swami's trip to America.

Touring the West

Persuaded by the views of Dewan of Porbandar and his friends at Madras, Swami Vivekananda set out on his journey to the USA on 31 May 1893 to attend the World Parliament of Religions in Chicago.

He reached Chicago much ahead of the commencement of the Parliament as none of his friends in India had ascertained the Parliament schedule. He reached Chicago on 28 July 1893 where as the commencement of the Parliament was on 11 September 1893, almost six weeks away. The date of registration as a delegate was long over and he had no letter or credentials from any society or organization. More over, he was not aware what religion he would represent at the Parliament, and most importantly he was short of money.

He was amazed and impressed by the material progress of America and thought about how much India still needed to acquire. Swami arrived in Chicago penniless and soon, due to shortage of money he was forced to shift to Boston where the cost of living was a little less. In Boston, he happened to meet Professor John Wright of Harvard University, who was a highly learned and a well known man in the social circle. The professor soon realized during his talks with Vivekananda, that he was an intellectual and spiritual soul. When Prof John Wright encouraged him to represent Hinduism in Chicago, Swami hesitated that he had no credentials. The professor instantly replied 'To ask you, Swami, for your credentials is like asking the Sun to state it's right to shine.' The professor immediately arranged for Swami's admission into the Chicago World Parliament of Religions by giving him enough money and references. He also arranged for his comfortable stay in Chicago.

In Chicago, he was invited to stay with Mrs. George. W. Hale where he was looked after very well. He was accompanied by the Hales to the venue of parliament of religions where he submitted his credentials and was accepted as a delegate. He was very grateful to the Hale family for having helped him in every possible way and soon they became his close friends.

On 11 September 1893, the Parliament of Religions opened. The gallery was packed with 7000 men and women. Among the delegates who took their seats in the huge hall, Swami Vivekananda was conspicuous in his ochre robe, yellow turban and a face that shone with divinity. He had no personal feelings except the feeling of carrying out an important mission that was entrusted to him by his guru, Sri Ramakrishna. He considered himself as a mere messenger of his Guru and of his motherland. He spent every moment before the session in prayer and meditation.

Swami Vivekananda
on the Platform of the Parliament of Religions

Swami's turn came in the afternoon. It was a great moment for him. As his name was announced, he stood up on the dias and bowed to Goddess Saraswati, before he started to speak. Surveying the great gathering, he began, 'Sisters and Brothers of America!' As he uttered these words, the entire assembly broke into loud applause which continued for two full minutes. These five simple words touched every heart that was present there, for those words did not represent any nation, religion, caste or creed. Their mere utterance spoke of universal brotherhood and entire audience gave a standing ovation as a tribute to the great man. An instant applause to an unknown Hindu monk represented a genuine acceptance of oneness of the entire mankind.

Swami's speech on the first day was brief but intense which captured the whole assembly. His powerful speech at the opening session of the Parliament brought him instant fame and acclaimed him as a great orator and the most ideal interpreter of India's wisdom. He instantly became very popular in America. The press, newspapers and popular men of America bestowed him with the finest of remarks. The New York Herald went to an extent of saying 'Vivekananda was undoubtedly the greatest figure in the Parliament of Religions; after hearing him we feel how foolish it is to send missionaries to this learned nation.' Thus, he earned fame not only for himself, he glorified India too.

In the Parliament of Religions, Vivekananda addressed the assembly more than a dozen times. The audience listened to his speeches in rapt attention and every time he finished speaking, the response was nothing but deafening applause. In all of his speeches, he stressed on universal tolerance and acceptance. He spoke to the audience about Hinduism and enlightened them with the gist of the religion. He emphasized that there is no need for any individual to convert from his religion to another because what every religion preaches is one and the same. Instead, he asked them to believe in oneness of the spirit, yet preserving their individuality. He leapt into fame with the sincerity in his messages and soon the streets of Chicago were filled with his life size picture with words 'The Monk Vivekananda' written beneath.Everyone who passed by, bowed their heads in reverence in front of his picture.

He made India proud. Indian magazines and newspapers published reports of the Parliament and the country men's hearts were filled with pride to see their fellow Indian conquer the world. The man himself, after delivering the first speech wept like a child after he returned to his hotel. He sensed that his life as a solitary monk in constant communication with God came to an end. He knew that he should put up with the turmoil of turning out into a public figure. But for India, he chose to take all the hardships that came his way. Now that he was famous, he was offered money, hospitality and all the luxuries in the world, but as a true Sannyasin he refused to sell religion for the sake of making money. He did not have any material wants. He did not care for name and fame. His only thought was to revive his mother land from the state of poverty and ignorance. He constantly prayed to Maa Durga to show him a way to save India and to raise the poor masses.

The impact of his lectures and wisdom was so high that, though all the other delegates in the parliament spoke during the session, everything they said and discussed were long forgotten by the world. But even nearly after 115 years of that Parliament session, the whole world remembers and cherishes the speeches of Swami Vivekanada and in fact, his speeches have become a reference point to many spiritual leaders, intellectuals and aspirants.

Years later, after the Parliament session, a Jewish intellectual remarked that he understood and realized his own religion, Judaism, only after he heard the lectures of Swami Vivekananda. He said that Swami addressed the world then, not only on behalf of his religion, but all the religions of the world. Such is his influence on the human race all over the world even today.

Soon after Parliament, he was invited to lecture in various parts of America. He spent only a little of the money he made from those lectures for his personal use, enough only to free himself from the obligation of his wealthy friends who were looking after him then. The remaining large chunk was sent to India to help various religious projects. He preached about the unity of faiths and scattered the seeds of purity, knowledge and faith all over the West.

He toured fourteen American cities to lecture, and mainly to remove preconceived and wrong notions about Hinduism from the minds of Americans. Due to his frequent touring, Americans called him 'Cyclonic Hindu'. His lectures forced Americans to change their view about India. Back in India, the news of his work and lectures created magic and instilled self confidence in the minds of numerous Indians. His efforts and success in the West had a revitalizing effect on India. Owing to him, India was then ready to search for her own identity and was also ready to create a special place for herself among all the countries of the world. He came like a breeze to revive India when she was gasping for breath.

After his lecture tour, he started free classes on Yoga and Vedanta in New York. Thousands of people came there to learn from him and finally a Vedanta society was founded in New York. After his stay in America for two years, he toured England and Europe too, where he was looked upon as a great master of Hindu religion. After the England tour, he came back to America and continued his classes in New York. Later, he left for Europe on a lecturing tour which was a huge success.

Till date, the people of the West claim that there would have been no other person worthier than Swami Vivekananda from India, who could bring about such wisdom to them and to their countries. Wherever he went, he and India were treated with reverence.

One day in America, Swami was watching some boys standing on a bridge trying to shoot at egg-shells that were floating on the river, but they always missed their target as the egg shells continuously bobbed up and down in the water. Swami continued to watch them with great interest to see if they could hit any of the shells. Meanwhile, the boys saw him watching them and they called out to Swami and asked him if he could hit the shells. Swami smiled and said he would try, took the gun and aimed at the shells. Though, he had never fired a gun before, he hit an egg shell all the twelve times he fired. Amazed at his aim, the boys asked Swami 'Well Mister, how did you do it? You must be a practiced hand.' Swami laughed and told them that he had never handled a gun before. He also told them 'Whatever you are doing, put your whole mind on it. The secret of success lies in the power of concentration. If you are shooting, your mind should be only on the target. Then you will never miss. If you are learning your lessons, think only of the lesson. In my country boys are taught to do this.' Even in such simple occasions, he never let India's virtues go unnoticed. Such was his devotion towards his motherland.

After Swami became well-known in America, he was once given a rousing reception at a railway station as he got down from a train. Suddenly, mistaking Swami to be an African American, a porter who was also African American, went forward, shook hands with him and said, 'Congratulations! I am extremely delighted that a man of my race has attained such great honour! The entire African American community in this country feels proud of you!' Swami in turn eagerly shook hands with the porter and said warmly, 'Thank you, brother!' He refused to deny he was an African American. Many a times, he was insulted, humiliated and refused entry into many hotels due to the suspicion that he was an African American. But he never protested or explained that he was Indian. A Western disciple once asked him why he did not tell them he was from India in such situations. Swami immediately replied, 'What? Rise at the expense of another! I did not come to earth for that!' The great man not only preached universal brotherhood but followed it too.

Back into the Mother's Lap

After three and half years of spiritual ministry in the West, he decided to return to India. Before he left England, one of his British friends asked him 'Swami, how do you like your motherland now after four years of the luxurious, glorious, powerful West?'

Swami replied, 'I loved India before I came away. Now the very dust and air of India are holy to me. It is now a holy land, the place of pilgrimage, the Tirtha.' Though Swami spoke of Hinduism, to him Indian nationalism was divine and it was also his greatest inspiration.

He reached Colombo on 15 January 1897, on his way to India. When news of his return to India spread, people from all over India prepared to give him a hero's welcome. Indeed he was a hero, who awakened the youth of India from a deep slumber. Once he stepped ashore at Colombo, thousands of people flung themselves on the ground to touch his feet. Aristocrats of Colombo welcomed him and took him in a grand procession. At Ramnad, the horses were released from his carriage and people of Ramnad, along with their Raja drew the carriage themselves. The Raja of Ramnad also erected a forty feet high victory tower at Rameswaram in the honour of Swami Vivekananda. From Colombo to Calcutta, he received an amazing and warm welcome at every city he passed by.

He received a fabulous welcome in Calcutta as well. He was greeted with intense enthusiasm; all the streets were decorated with bright lights. The people crowded along the roads of the city to have a glimpse of Swami. Soon after his arrival in Calcutta, Sri Ramakrishna's birth anniversary was celebrated in Dakshineswar. He took part in those celebrations along with his disciples. When he reached Dakshineswar, he was overwhelmed with mixed emotions of nostalgia, joy and grief to be back at that holy place. He wandered bare foot all over the place, visited temples, his master's room and all the places which brought back memories of his master.

On 1 May 1897, Swami Vivekananda gathered all the devotees of Sri Ramakrishna and emphasized the need to organize their work in a more systematic manner.

He gave them insight about our shortcomings and also the organized methods of American functioning. He appealed to every monk and every devotee, that India's intelligence, energy and efforts should be more channelised to attain the mission of uplifting the masses. To put his thoughts into action more systematically, Ramakrishna Mission Association was founded. It had two departments of action – Indian and Foreign. While the Indian section looked after the training of monks and devotees, establishing monasteries, etc, the Foreign department sent the trained devotees to other countries to start centres there and to spread the teachings of the Master worldwide. Thus, Swami's vision of employing religion for mankind's welfare was realized.

Within a few weeks of founding the mission, one of Swami's brother disciples was passing through a place in Bengal where he found people suffering from acute famine. He was struck by their suffering and immediately started relief work on behalf of the mission. Since then Ramakrishna Mission also started providing relief to those people who suffered from natural and man-made calamities.

The small centre which was managed by the other monks while Swami Vivekananda was touring the West was transferred to Belur after his return to India. It was

Belur Math

named Belur Math, which became the headquarters of the Ramakrishna Mission. The architecture of the Belur Math is modern and unique in its own way. It symbolizes universal brotherhood and oneness of all the religions. The shrine resembles a temple, a mosque and a church, when seen from different angles. During the construction of the shrine at Belur, it is believed that Swami Vivekananda incorporated many ideas he derived from several monuments, palaces and places of architectural value like the Taj Mahal, temples of Rajasthan, Gujarat and Tamil Nadu when he travelled

India and the West. The Ramakrishna Mission proclaims the Belur Math is a 'A Symphony in Architechture.'

Another ashram known as the 'Advaita Ashrama' was founded by Swami in 1899 at Mayavati on the Himalayas, near a place called Almora. It is now one of the most important publication centres of the Ramakrishna Math, Ramakrishna Mission and the Belur Math.

Swami's long term vision was to build a University as a part of the Ramakrishna Mission. His main focus was always education. One of his dedicated disciples from the West was Margaret E. Noble, an Irish woman, whom Swami considered his spiritual daughter. She renounced her mother land and western ways of life to dedicate herself to the cause of the Mission. Swami Vivekananda later named her Nivedita, which means 'dedicated'. As a first step towards her commitment to the mission, she opened Nivedita School in Calcutta in November 1898.

By now Swami had become a messiah for the whole world. He visited Europe again in 1899 along with Nivedita and another disciple after consolidating all the activities he started in India. He stayed for a short while in England and then left to New York where he stayed only for few months. He moved on to California to lecture there. At the end of his lectures, a Vedanta society was founded in San Francisco. He went to Paris and stayed there for three months where he participated in the Congress of History of Religions. This was his last trip to the West and he returned to India after monitoring the progress of his work in that part of the world. He returned to India in December 1900 and spent most of his time in the Belur math participating actively in the training activities of the aspirant monks and in guiding the mission in spreading its presence all over the world.

Journey to the Heavenly Abode

It was Swami's self prophecy that he would not live to be forty years old. Accordingly, he left this world on 4 July 1902 after a busy day at the Belur math. He taught Veda to some pupils in the morning on that day and also had a walk with one of his brother disciple. During the walk, he gave the brother disciple instructions regarding the future of the Ramakrishna math. He passed away in meditation that evening. He was only thirty nine years and five months old when he left his physical abode. His disciples say that he attained Mahasamadhi. Though the doctors claim that the death was due to the rupture of a blood vessel in the brain, they could not ascertain the exact cause of his death.

As the news of his death spread, there was gloom all over the world. The monks and the monasteries felt desolated and the world was suddenly orphaned. It was again the words of Swami: 'May I be born again and again, and suffer thousands of miseries, so that I may worship the only God that exists, the only God I believe in, the sum of total souls', which rang in the ears of the his followers and got them back to their feet to carry on the mission of their great master.

Swami left behind him spiritual awareness, religious tolerance and spirit of oneness. Before he left, he prepared the world to continue the mission of establishing an equal and educated society, a mission he started with reverence. He was the man who taught the mankind to live the truth and to realize the light within one's soul.

He was the one who had experienced in his life, all the truths about which he spoke. He lived an accomplished life to its fullest. He lived to make the lives of the people around him more worthy. He always said, 'Life is a boon granted by God to each one of us. Don't fritter it way. Do not think you are worthless. Live a life of courage, happiness and peace.'

Another important message of Swami to the world was to 'Take up one idea. Make that idea your life—think of

Vivekananda Temple on Vivekananda rock at Kanyakumari, India

it, dream of it, live on that idea. Let the brain, muscles, nerves, every part of your body, be full of that idea, and just leave every other idea alone. This is the way to success, and this is the way great spiritual giants are produced.' He gave such valuable messages to the world and opened the gates of harmonious living to those who heard and followed him. His lectures are prized possessions of the world today.

Death cannot take a great man who inspired mankind away from this world. One who reads his works and understands the essence of his messages is sure to become a brave man who can face his life with confidence. Burden and despair in the heart will slowly slip away and make way for confidence and faith. He left priceless quotes and valuable messages in the form of lectures to raise the spirit of the mankind. Though, each message he gave to the world was unique in its own way, there are a few quotes which inspired and still continue to inspire millions around the world.

Priceless Pearls of Wisdom

- *The world is the great gymnasium where we come to make ourselves strong.*

- *We are what our thoughts have made us; so take care about what you think. Words are secondary. Thoughts live; they travel far.*

- *You cannot believe in God until you believe in yourself.*

- *All the powers in the universe are already ours. It is we who have put our hands before our eyes and cry that it is dark.*

- *The earth is enjoyed by heroes'—this is the unfailing truth. Be a hero. Always say, 'I have no fear.'*

- *Do not look back upon what has been done. Go ahead!*

- *Experience is the only teacher we have. We may talk and reason all our lives, but we shall not understand a word of truth until we experience it ourselves.*

- *Fill the brain with high thoughts, highest ideals, place them day and night before you, and out of that will come great work.*

- *Strength is life, weakness is death. Strength is felicity, life eternal, immortality. Weakness is constant strain and misery, death.*

- *First, believe in the world — there is meaning behind everything.*

- *Everything can be sacrificed for truth, but truth cannot be sacrificed for anything.*

- *Stand up, be bold, be strong. Take the whole responsibility on your own shoulders, and know that you are the creator of your own destiny.*

- *Knowledge can only be got in one way, the way of experience. There is no other way to know.*

- *Condemn none: if you can stretch out a helping hand, do so. If you cannot, fold your hands, bless your brothers, and let them go their own way.*

- *The greatest religion is to be true to your own nature. Have faith in yourselves!*

The Mission Continues

Swami Vivekananda largely influenced the youth of the world. He induced *shraddha* and selflessness into the minds of future aspirants. A great number of 20th century leaders have acknowledged that they have been influenced greatly by the works of Swami. He also is considered to have inspired the Indian Freedom Struggle. His writings instilled faith and courage in the minds of most of our freedom fighters to face the challenges our nation faced during the pre-independence era. Great personalities of India reverently acknowledged his influence on them.

Gandhiji, the father of the nation said 'After going through his works thoroughly, the love I have for this country has grown by thousand fold'.

Vivekananda

Rabindranath Tagore, a poet laureate proudly told the world, 'If you want to know India, study Vivekananda.' He said that Vivekananda, through his work, marked the awakening of a man in the fullness and influenced the youth to work towards liberation.

S.Radhakrishnan, former president of India, who was also a philosopher, said 'Vivekananda saved Hinduism and he gave us hope in distress and courage in despair.'

According to Subhash Chandra Bose, another freedom fighter, 'Vivekananda is the maker of Modern India.'

It is also very amazing to know that the basic principles on which UNESCO functions—tolerance, uplifting the downtrodden masses, advocating universal brotherhood, need for education, etc—have remarkable similarities to what Swami Vivekananda proposed almost a century ago. This only shows what an original thinker Swami was and how distant his was vision to establish a uniform society.

Above all, Sri Ramakrishna, Vivekananda's spiritual master acclaimed 'Some of my devotees are lotuses with ten petals, some like lotuses with sixteen petals, some like lotuses with a hundred petals. Vivekananda belongs to a very high plane. Among lotuses, he is a lotus with thousand petals.'

Sri Ramakrishna foresaw that the boy Naren would become a saviour of Indian future. There were millions of people who were deeply influenced by his teachings and work. They chose to follow every word he said and every step he took. The result of such an influence on the youth lead to the foundation of many missions, ashrams, charitable trusts and societies which work incessantly to accomplish the work given to them by Swami. As a mark of respect to the great man, his birthday, 12 January every year is observed as National Youth Day.

Today, there are numerous branches of the Ramakrishna Mission all over the world. All of them play a great role in establishing social equality and tirelessly work for the upliftment of the poor. The Mission has its own hospitals, charitable dispensaries, training centres, mobile dispensaries, maternity clinics, orphanages, old age homes, libraries and educational institutions.

All these organizations aim at achieving one goal—rescue of the poor and the destitute. They never say 'No' to anyone in need. They believe that 'God exists in the common man who is ignorant, a man who is nearing his death due to absence of medical facilities and a man who is starving but has no money to feed himself.' Most importantly, they follow their belief. For them the priority is not singing bhajans and devotional songs - it is seva to those who are in need of it. Seva includes providing education too.

Swami's call to the world was 'Arise! Awake! And stop not till the goal is reached.' He wanted every man to awaken his inner self and realise the beauty within him. His aim was to wake us up from the world of Maya or illusion and shake off the laziness. He emphasized on how important it is to have a goal and how very important it is to pursue the goal relentlessly till we achieve it. After all, an aimless life is a wasted itself. No man who comes in contact with the power of his teachings and his quotes, can ever escape the gush of positive energy flowing through him to tell him what he is worthy of.

Another lesson to learn from his life is 'humility'. Though a great man himself, he never let the accolades he won shake his roots. He was humble and was always a true disciple of his master Sri Ramakrishna till his last breath. He claimed that he achieved what he could and became what he was only due to his Guru, Sri Ramakrishna – 'If there has ever been a word of truth, a word of spirituality, that I have spoken anywhere in the world, I owe it to my Master; only mistakes are mine... Remember, it is His will – I'm a voice without a form.'

Now, we need to acknowledge that the world today is what it is only because of this selfless, great, passionate, patriotic saint, Swami Vivekananda. He continues to live in every child's dream for education. He lives in every man's will to find God in another man. He lives in each and every one of us, waiting to be recognized and realized.

———